Dtp
graphic design
photographer

by
I. Ad.

Girls

A study about girls in art

ISBN-13 : 978-1461019978
ISBN-10 : 1461019974

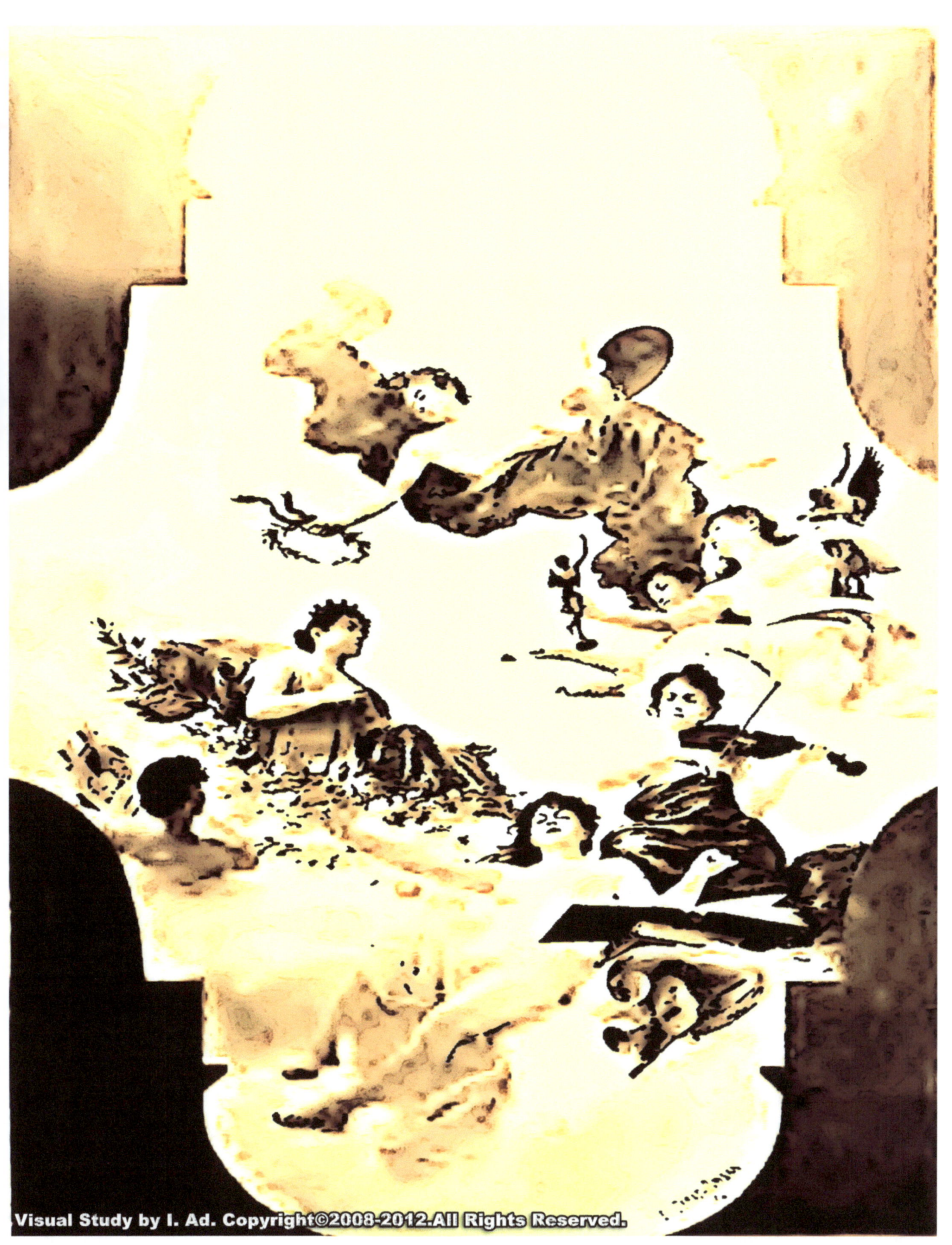

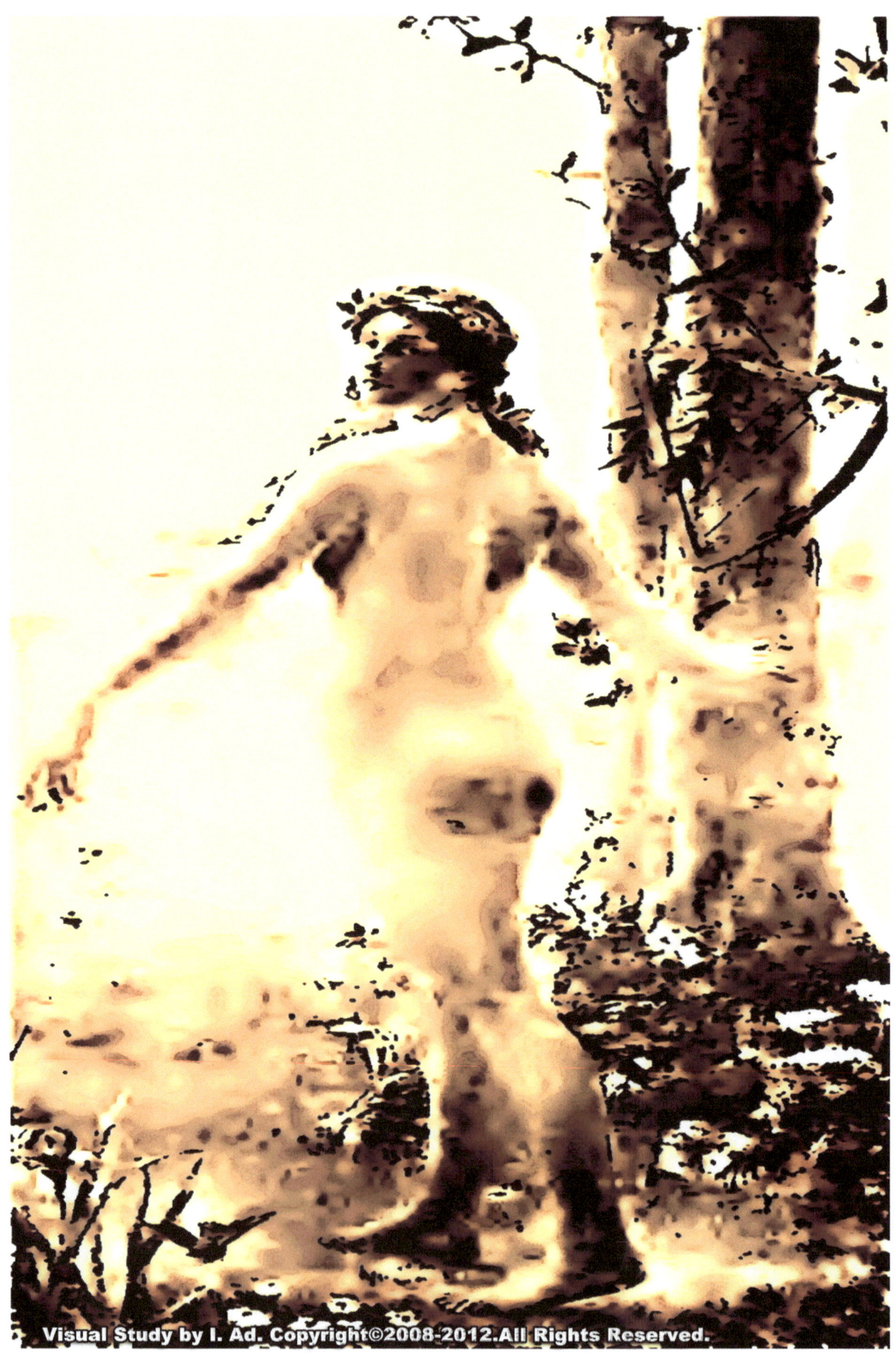

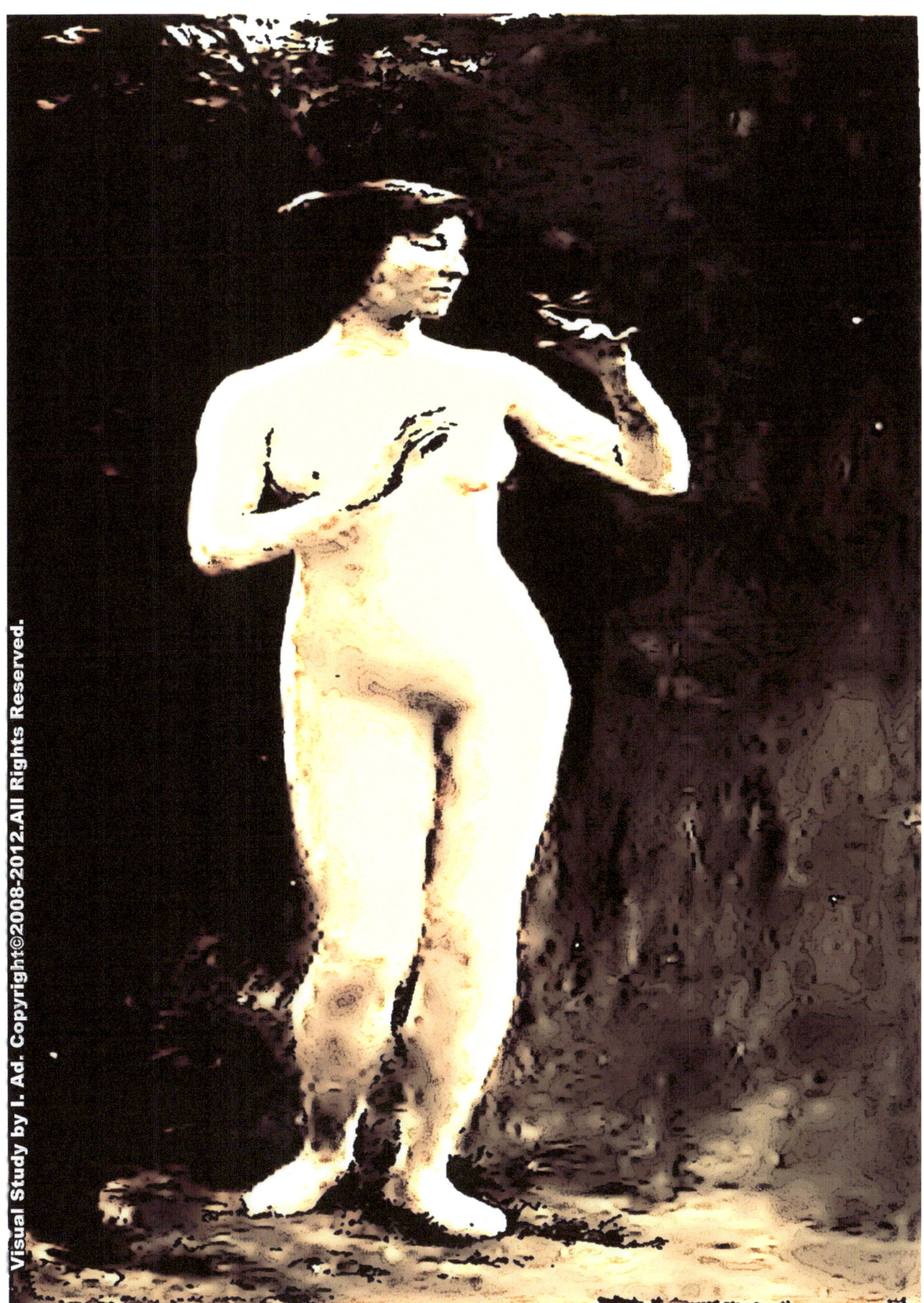

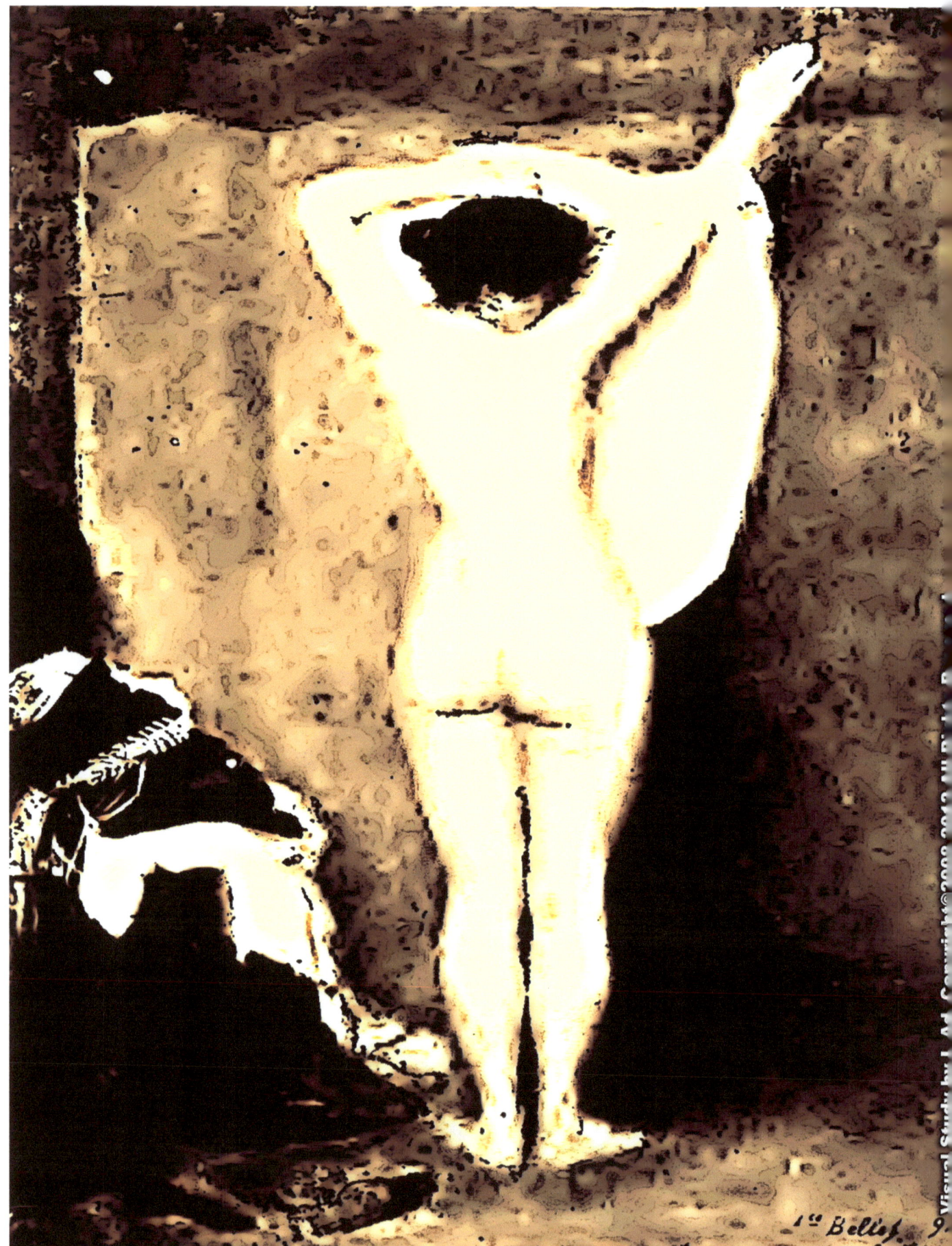

1st Belief 9

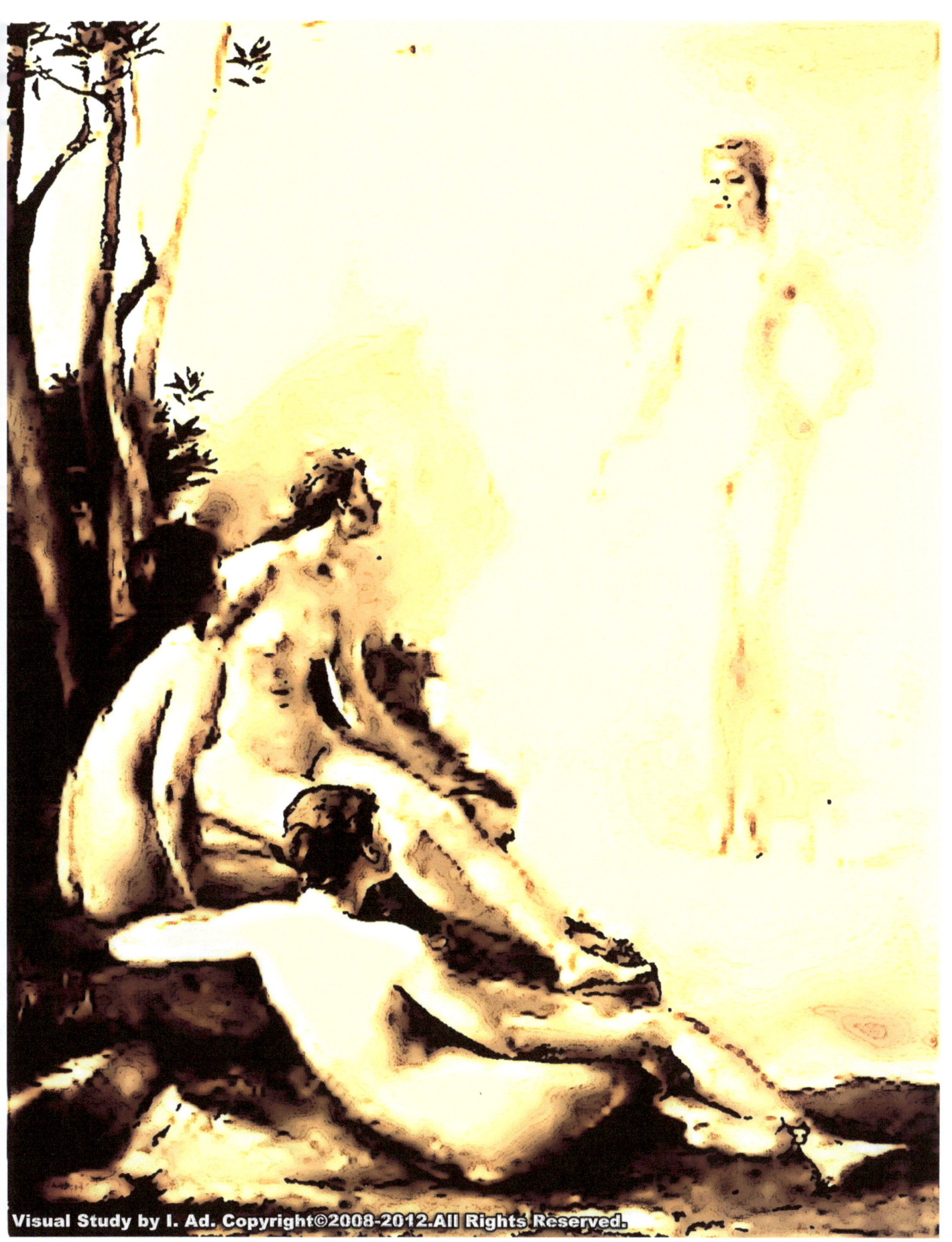

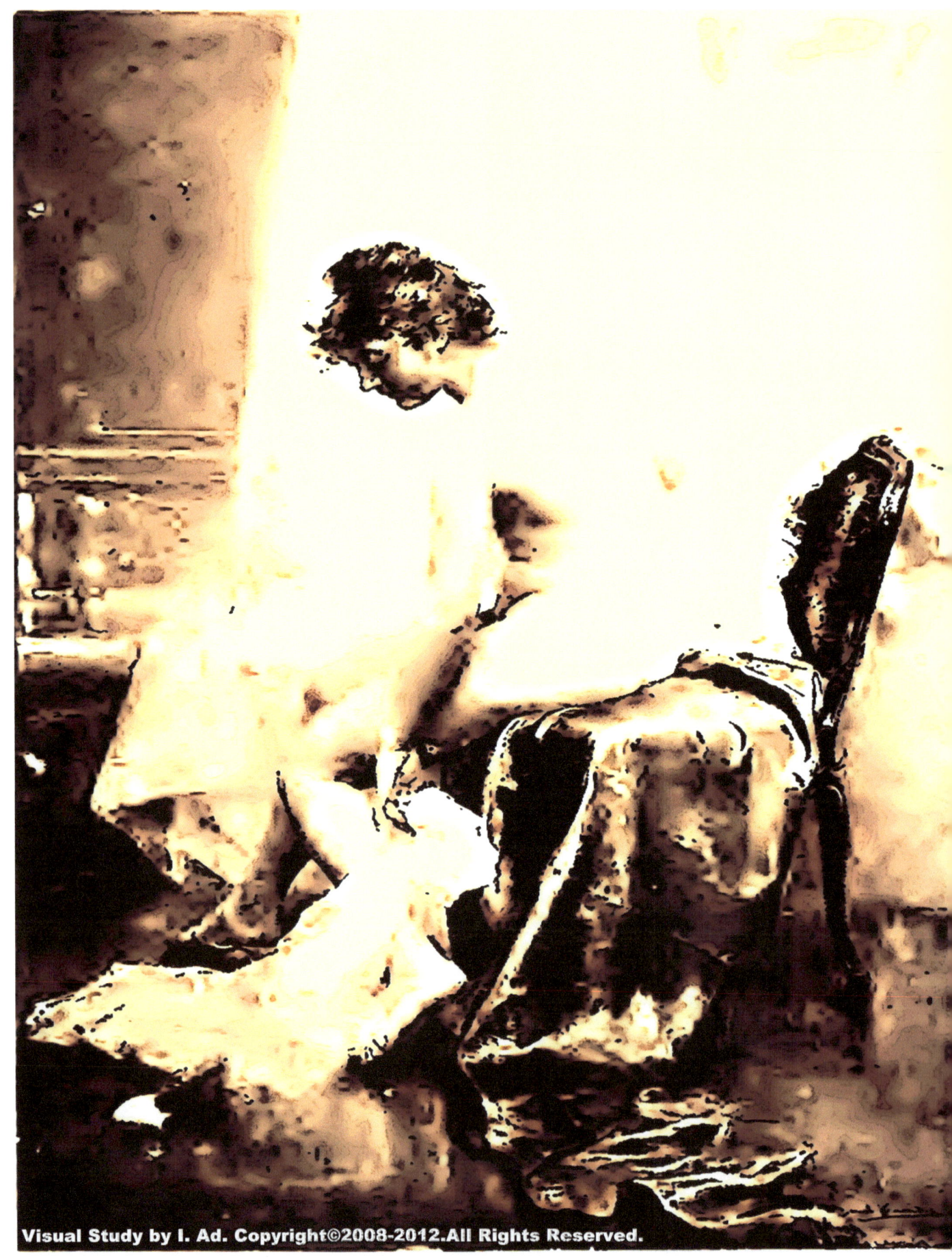

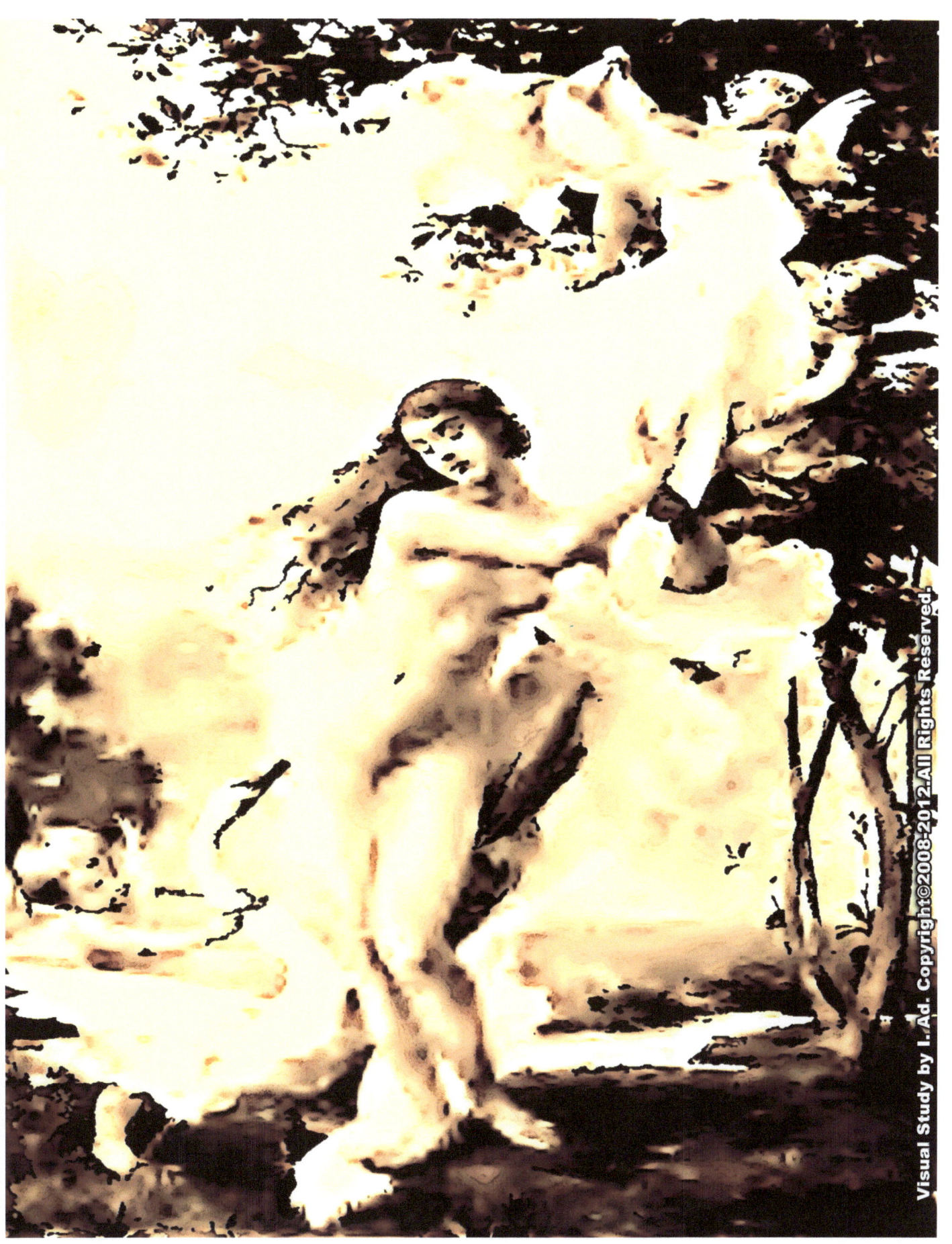

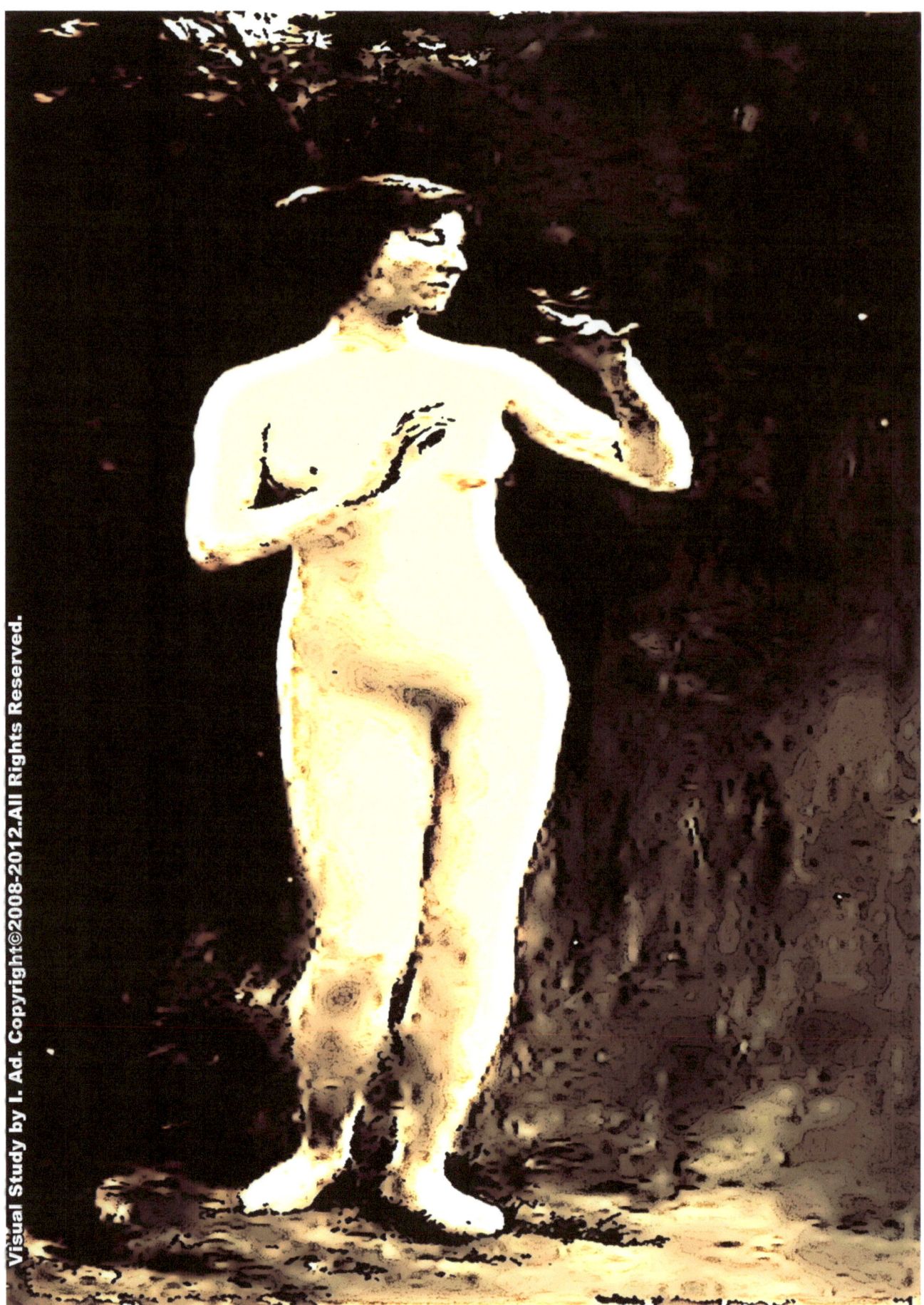

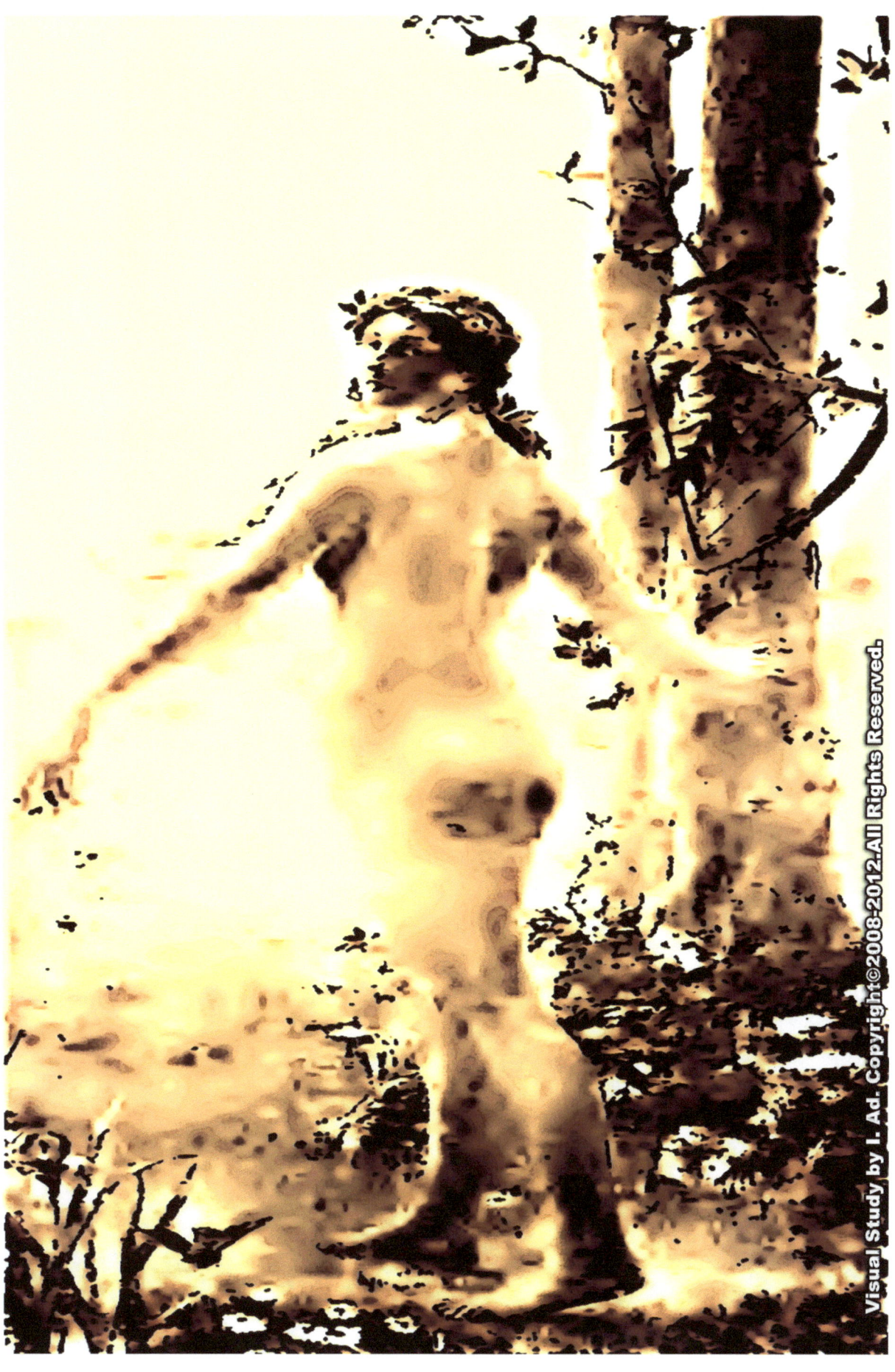

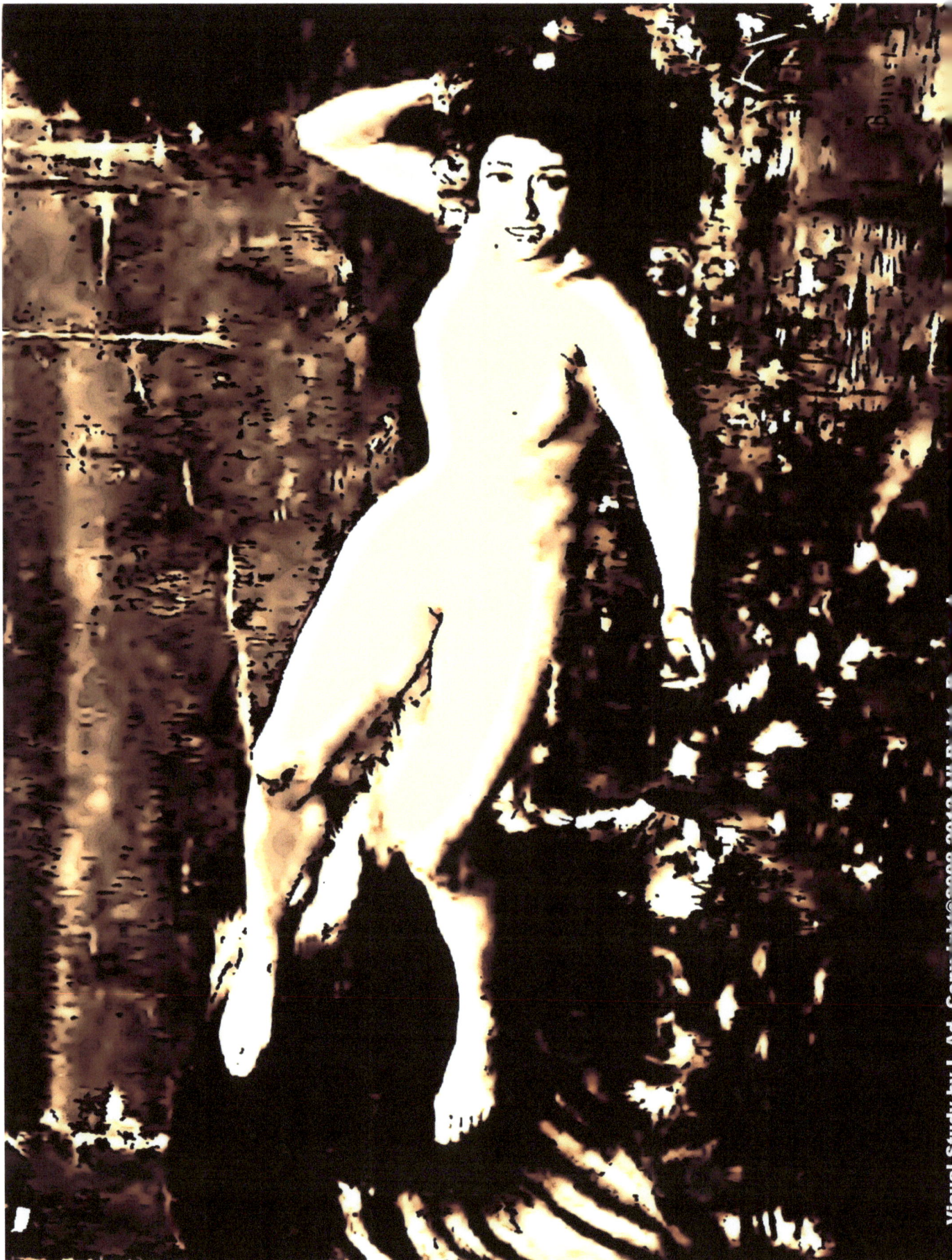

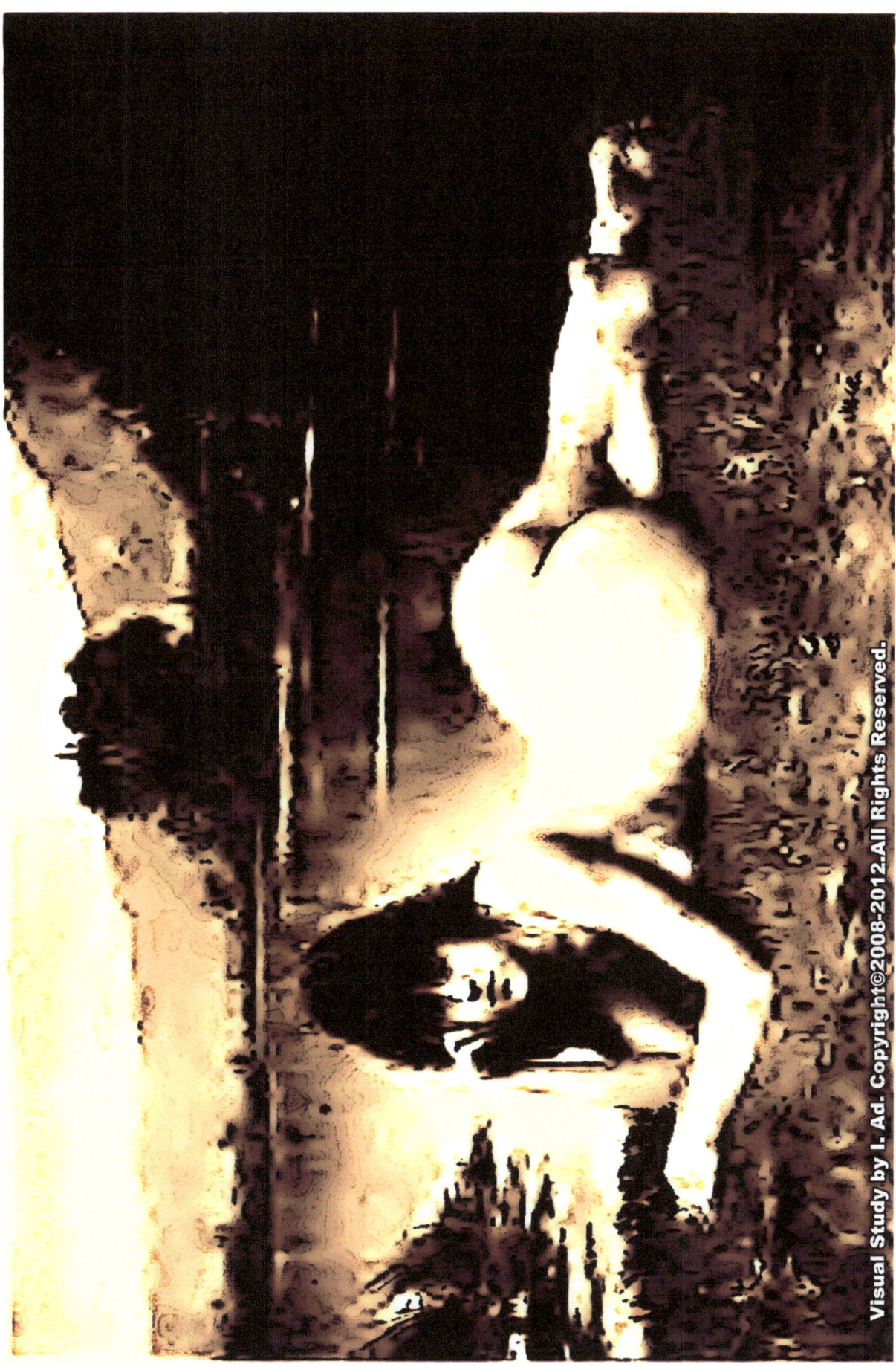

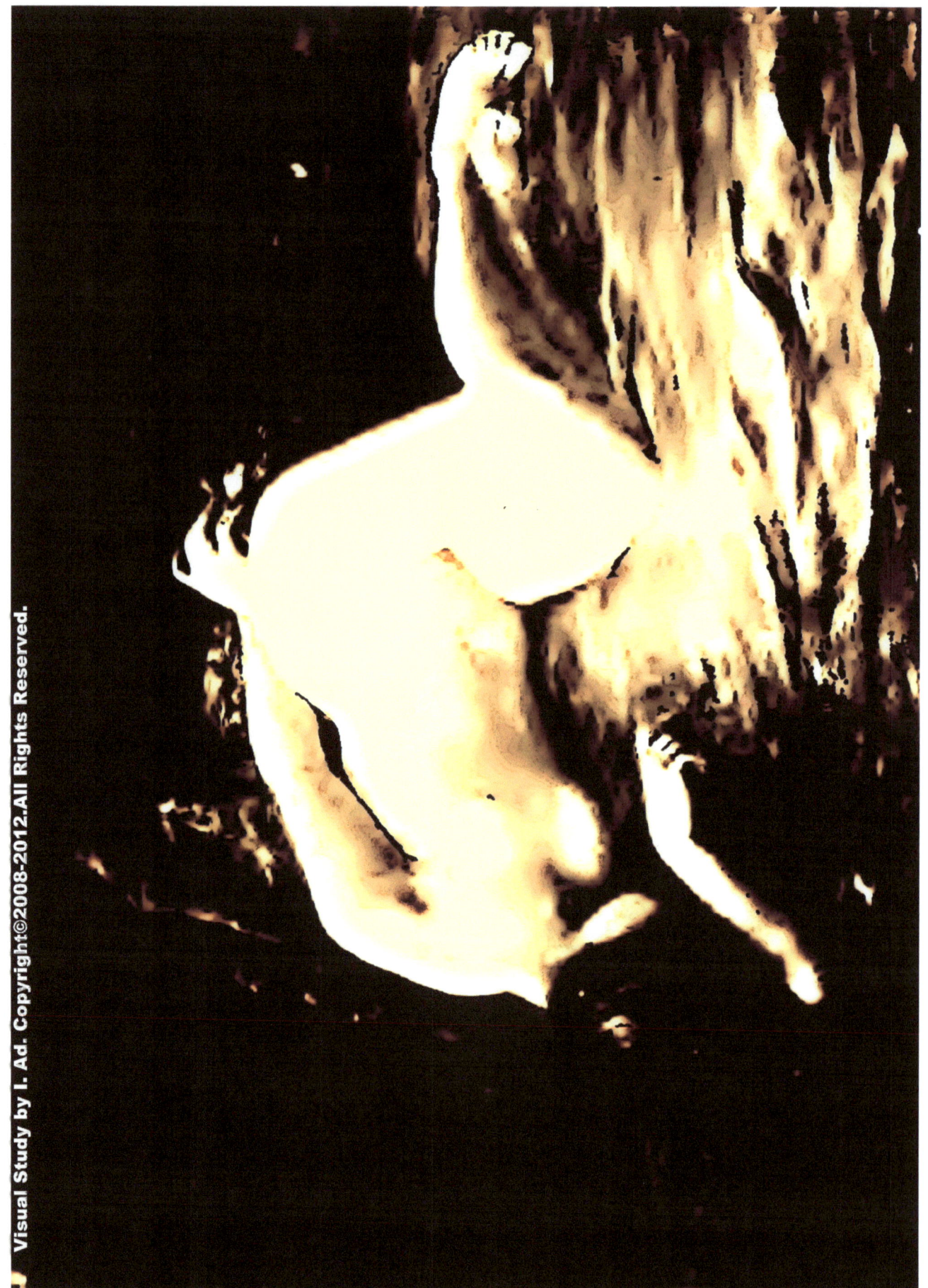

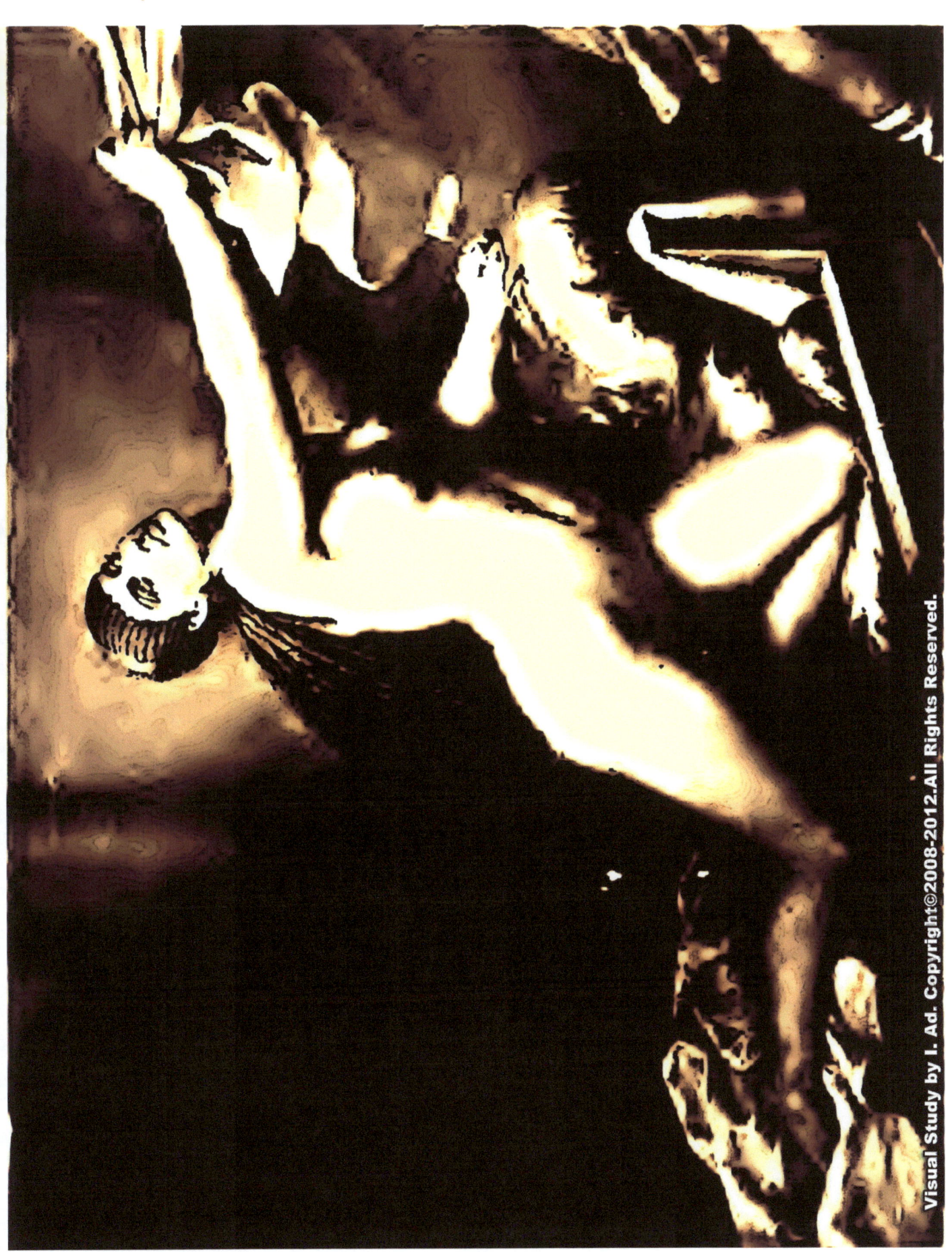

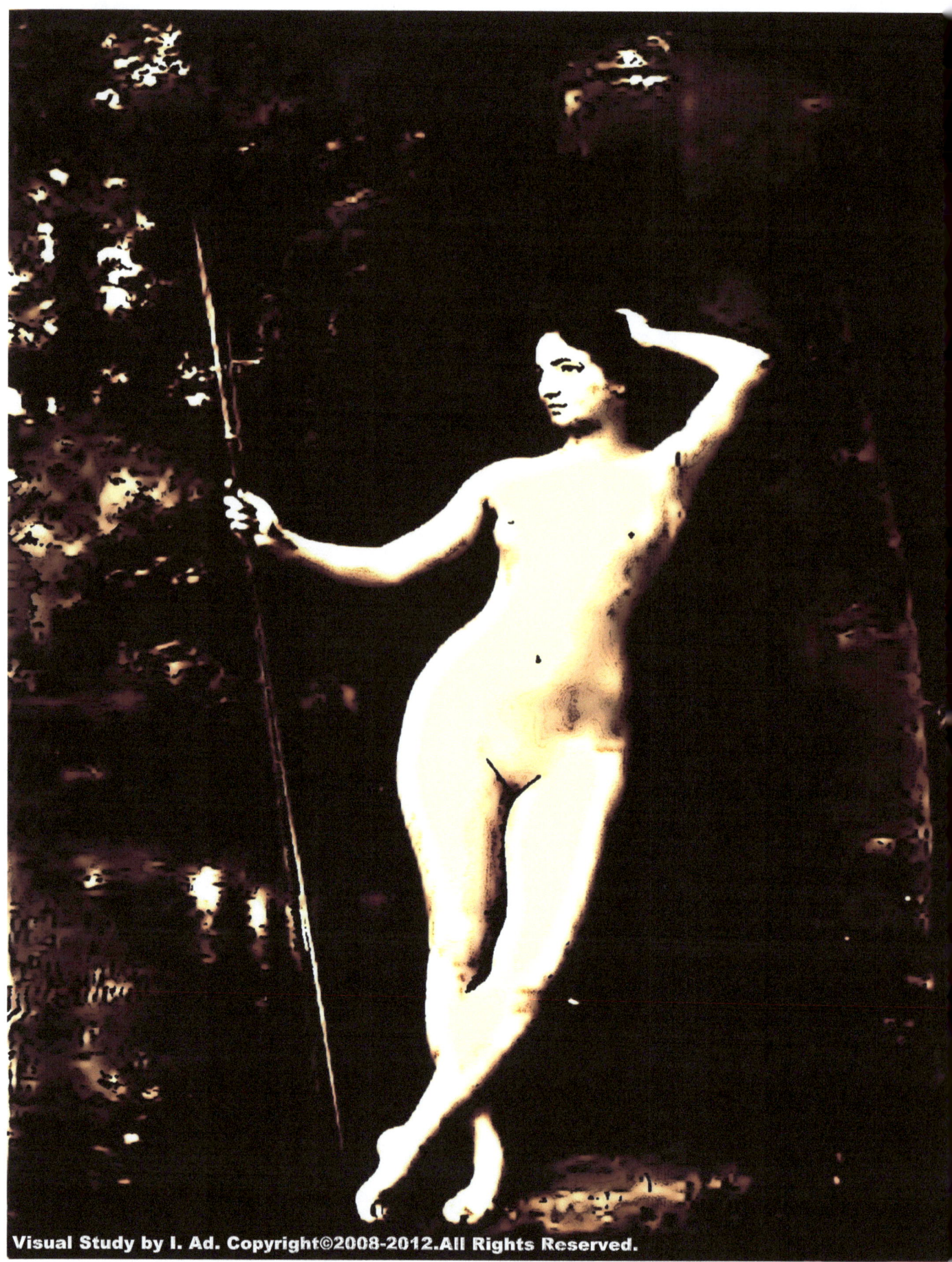

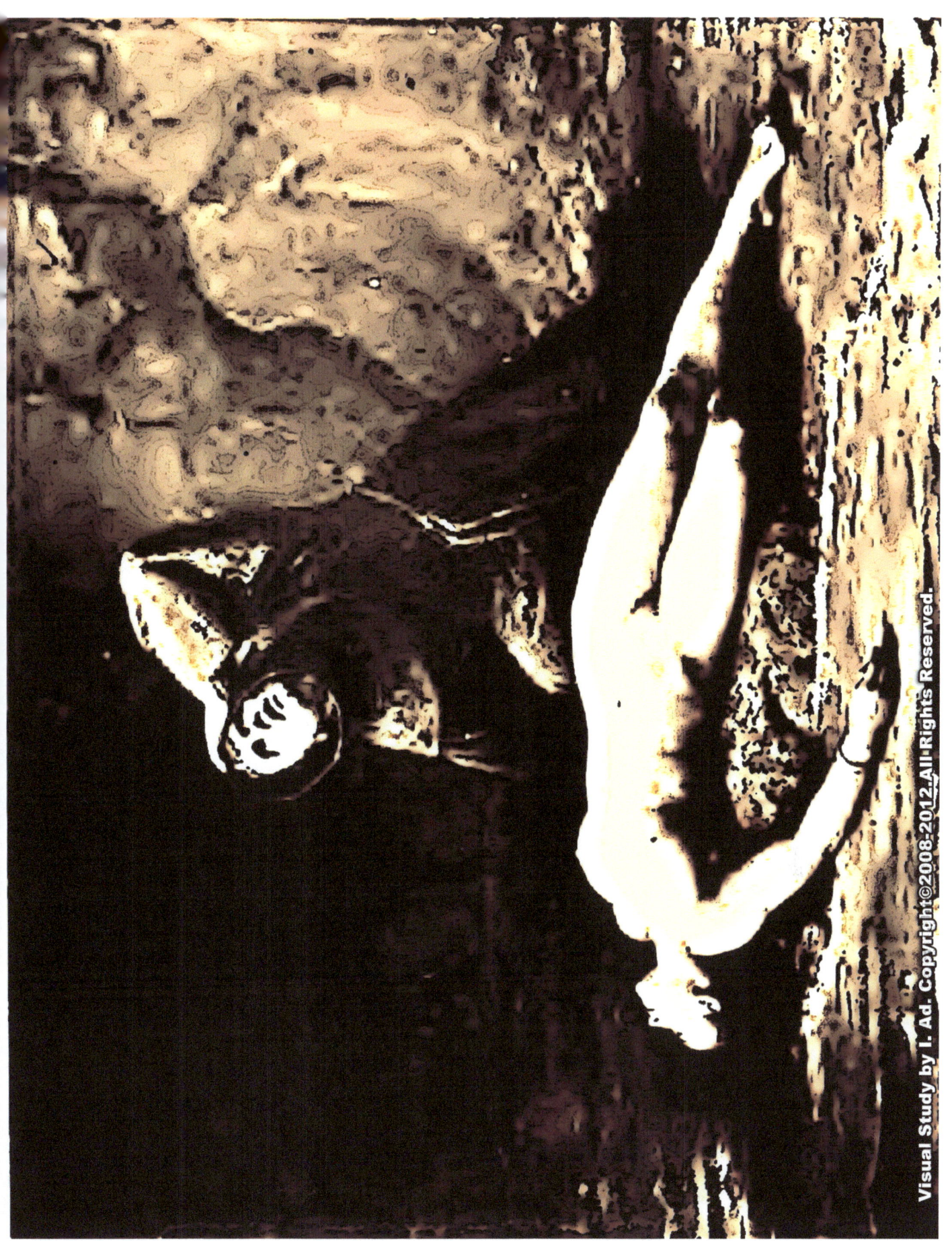

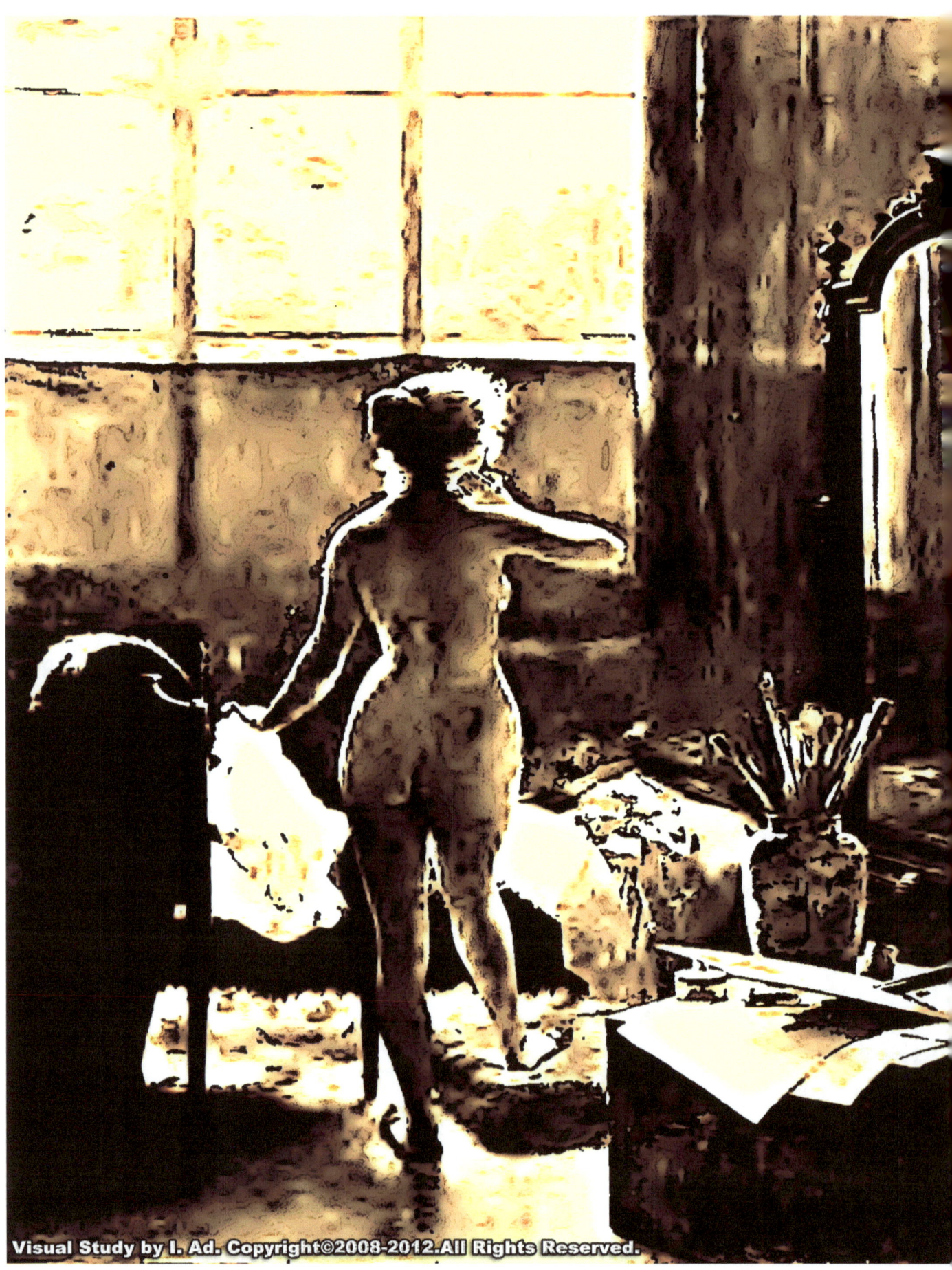

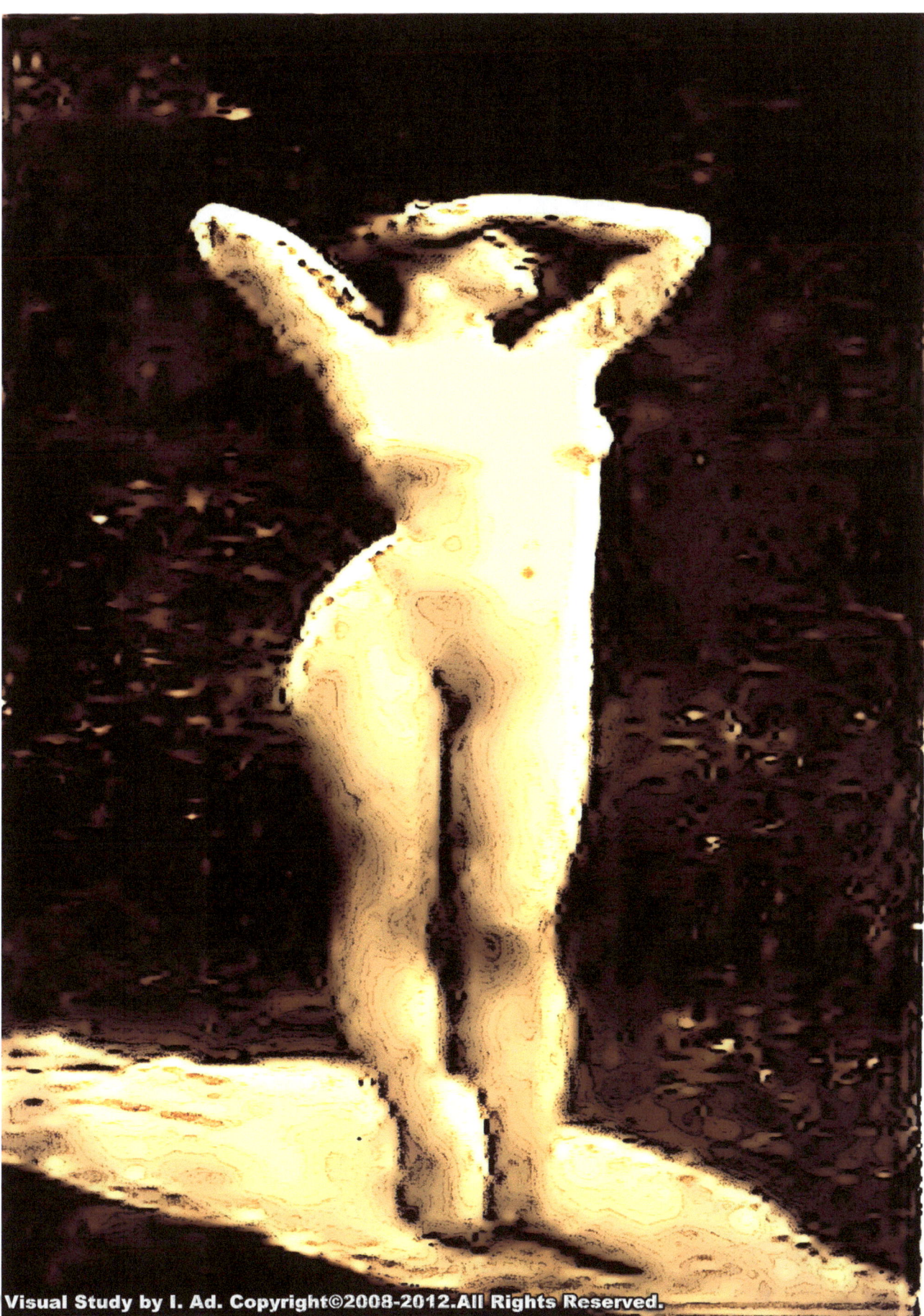

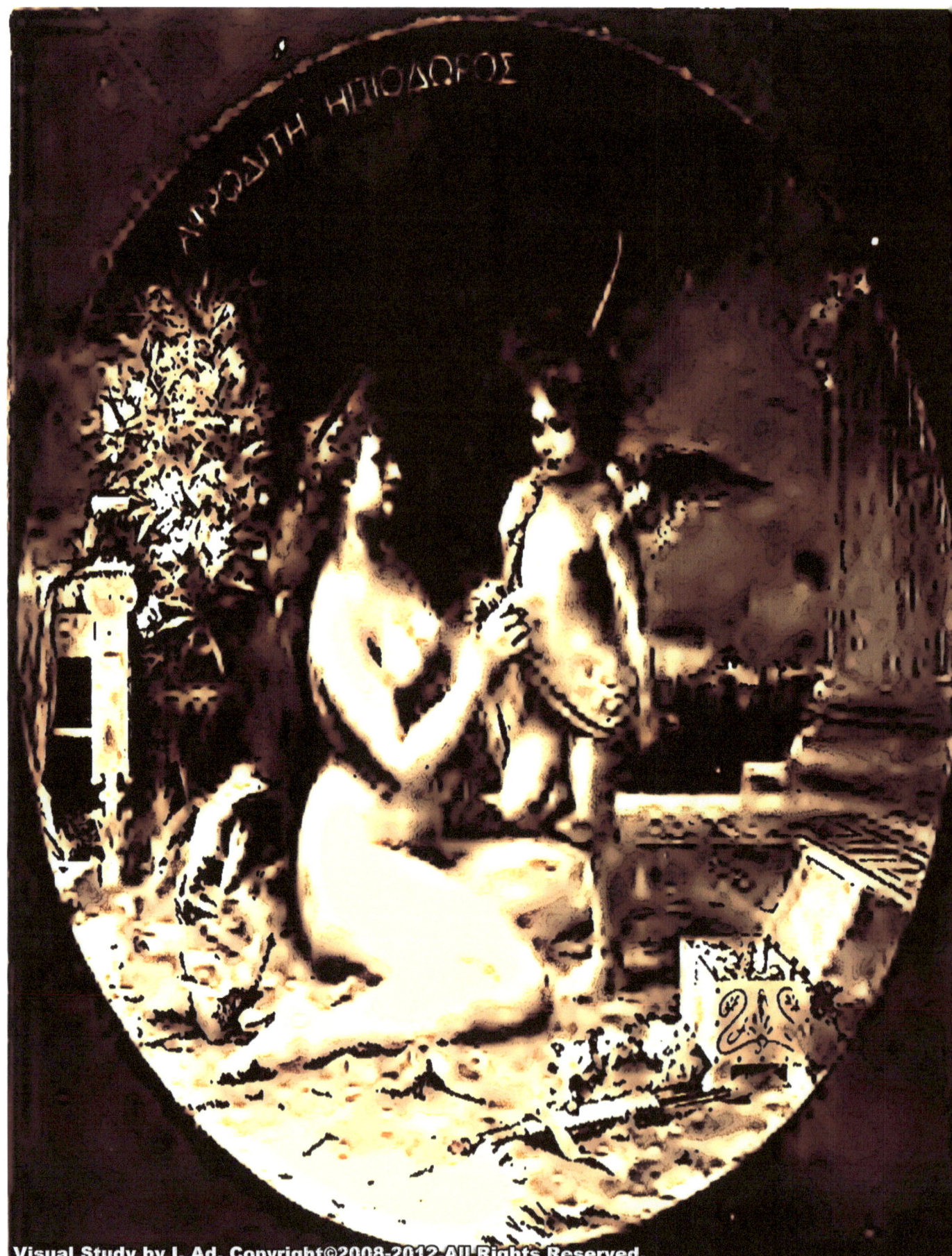

ΑΦΡΟΔΙΤΗ ΗΠΙΟΔΩΡΟΣ

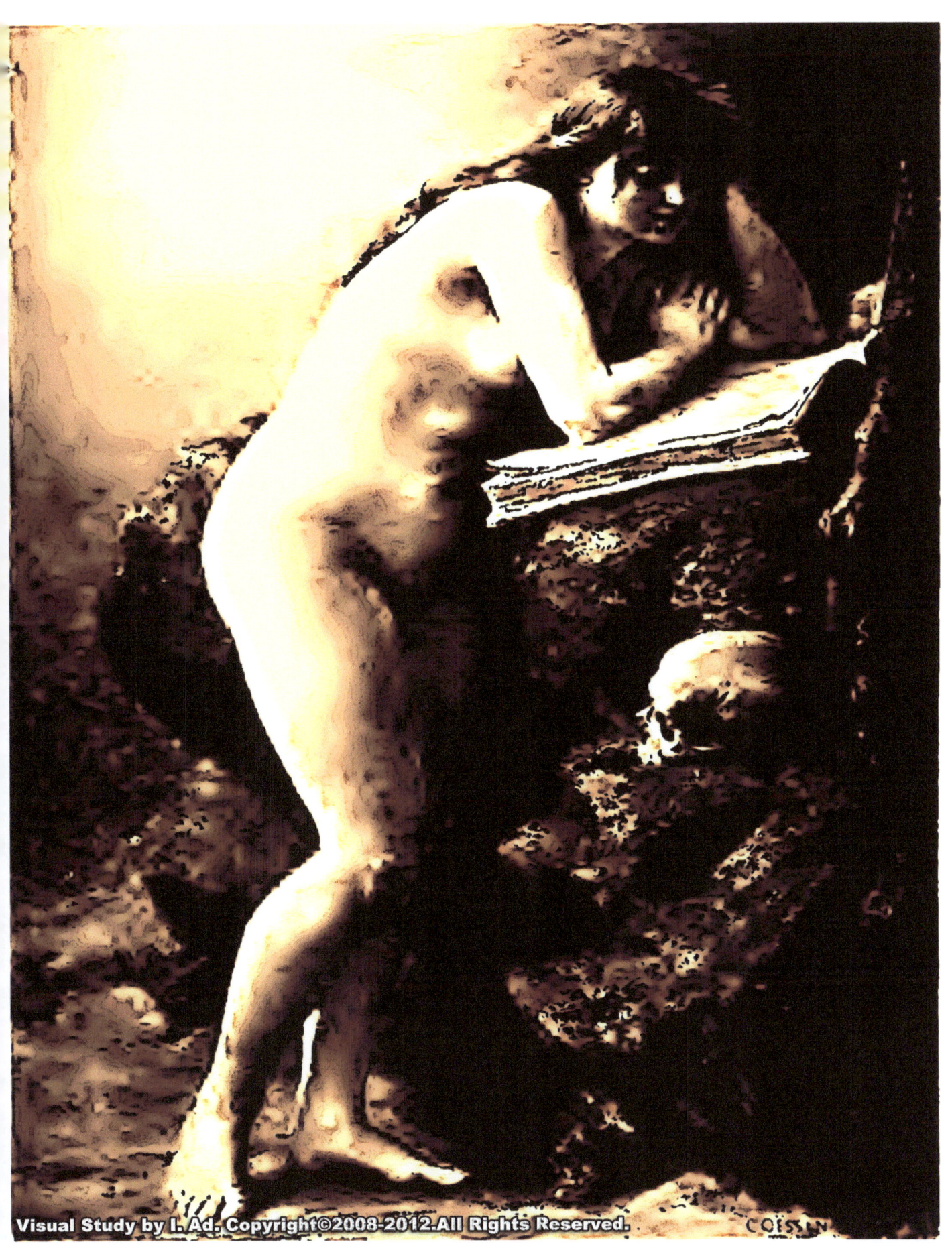

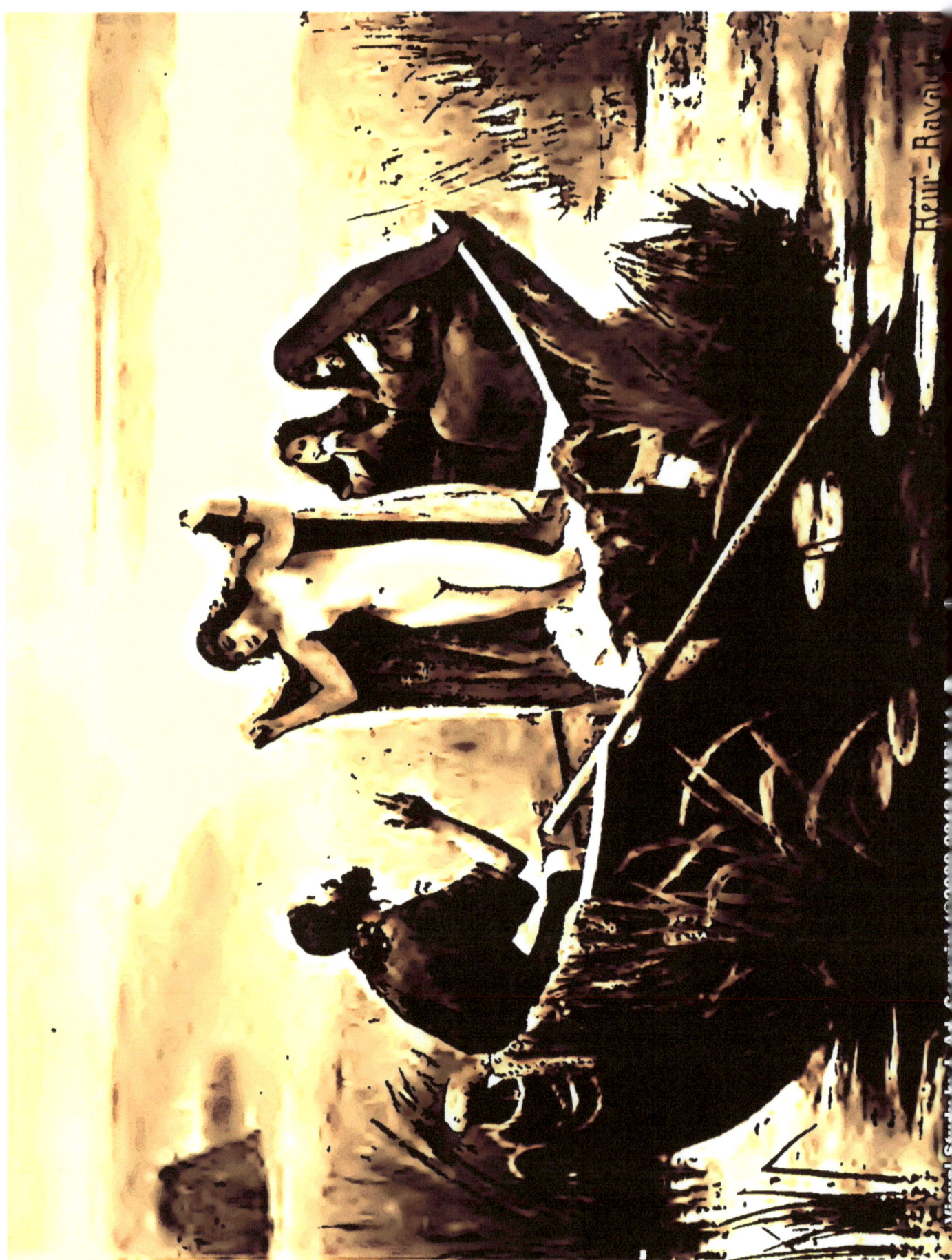

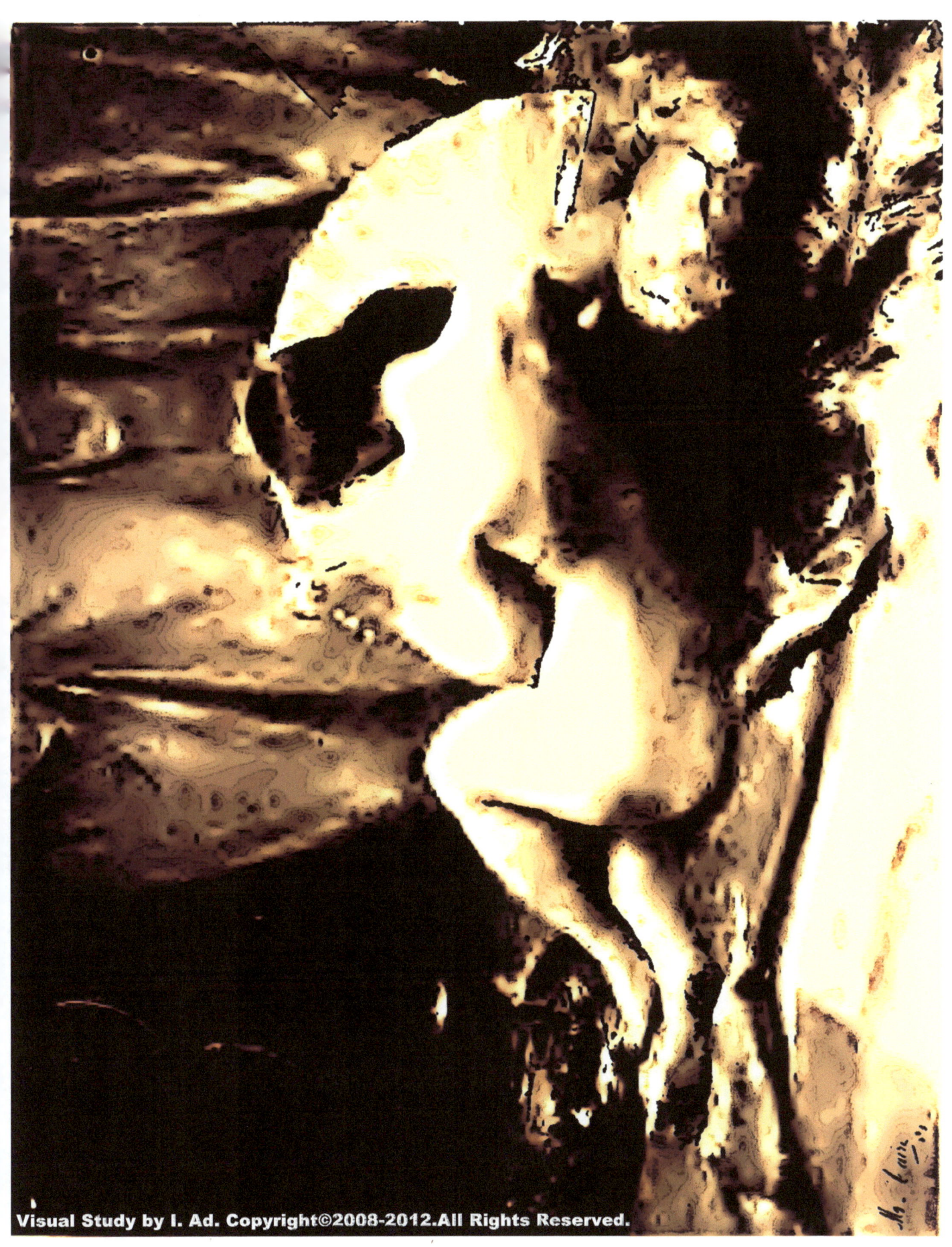

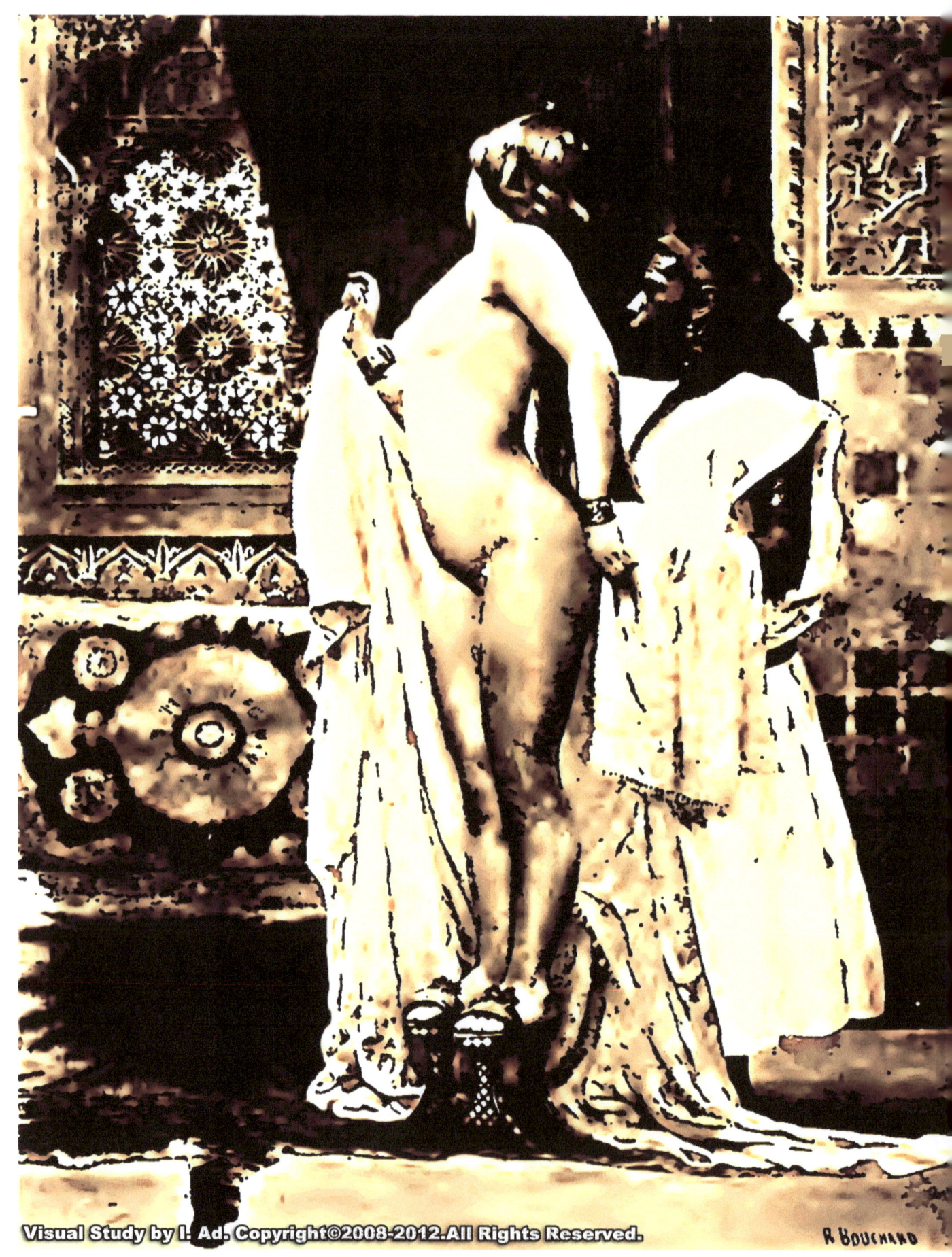

R BOUCHARD

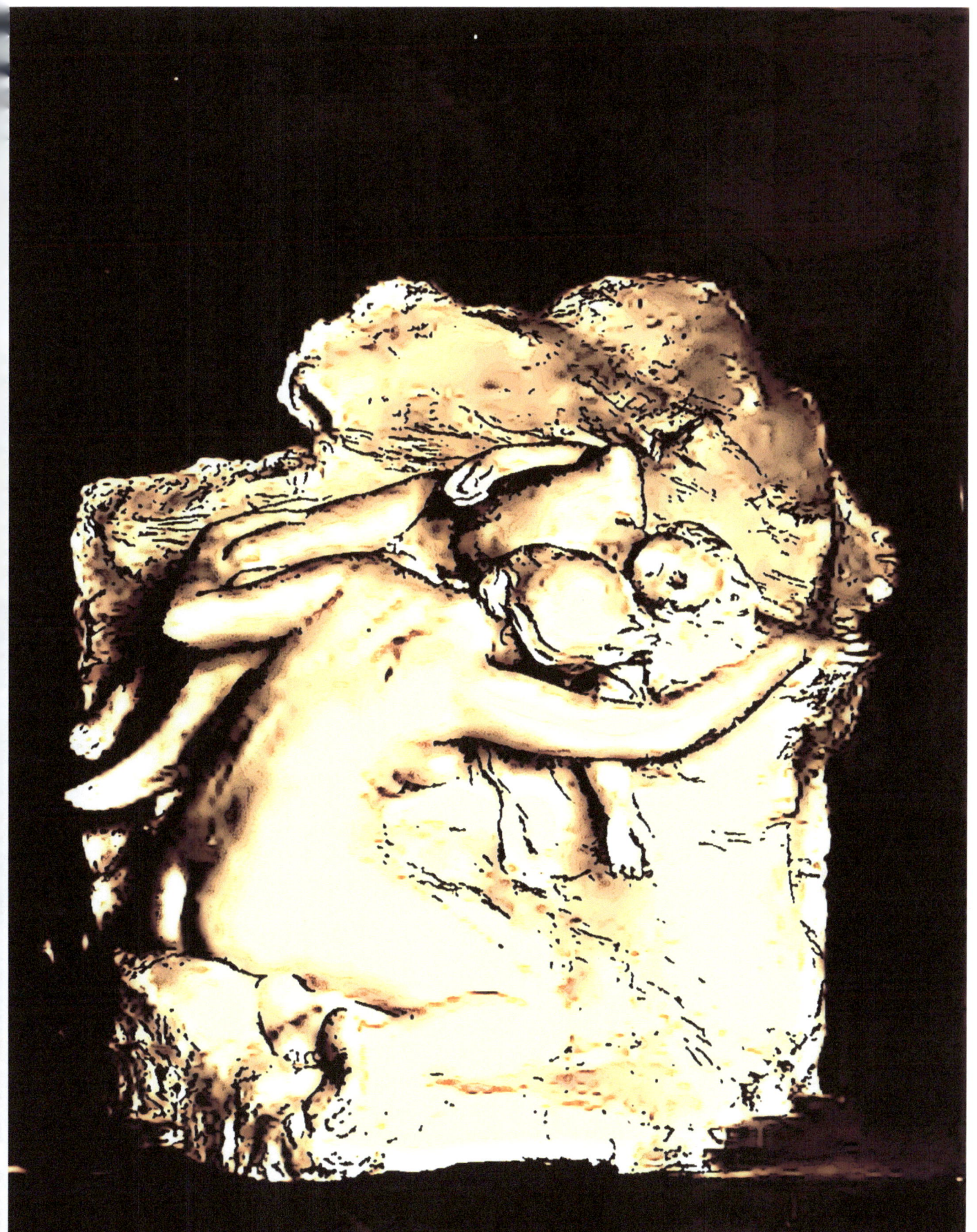

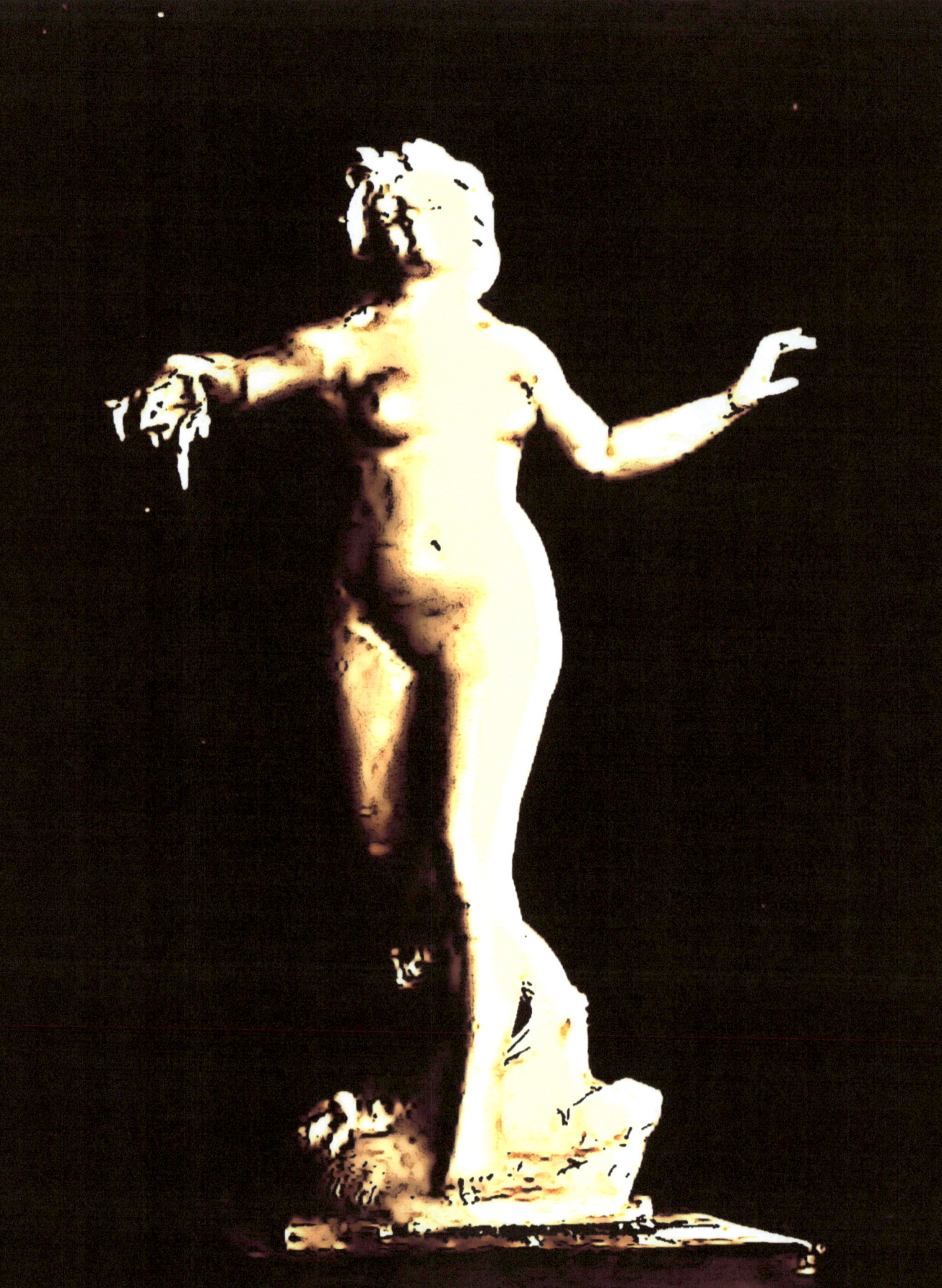

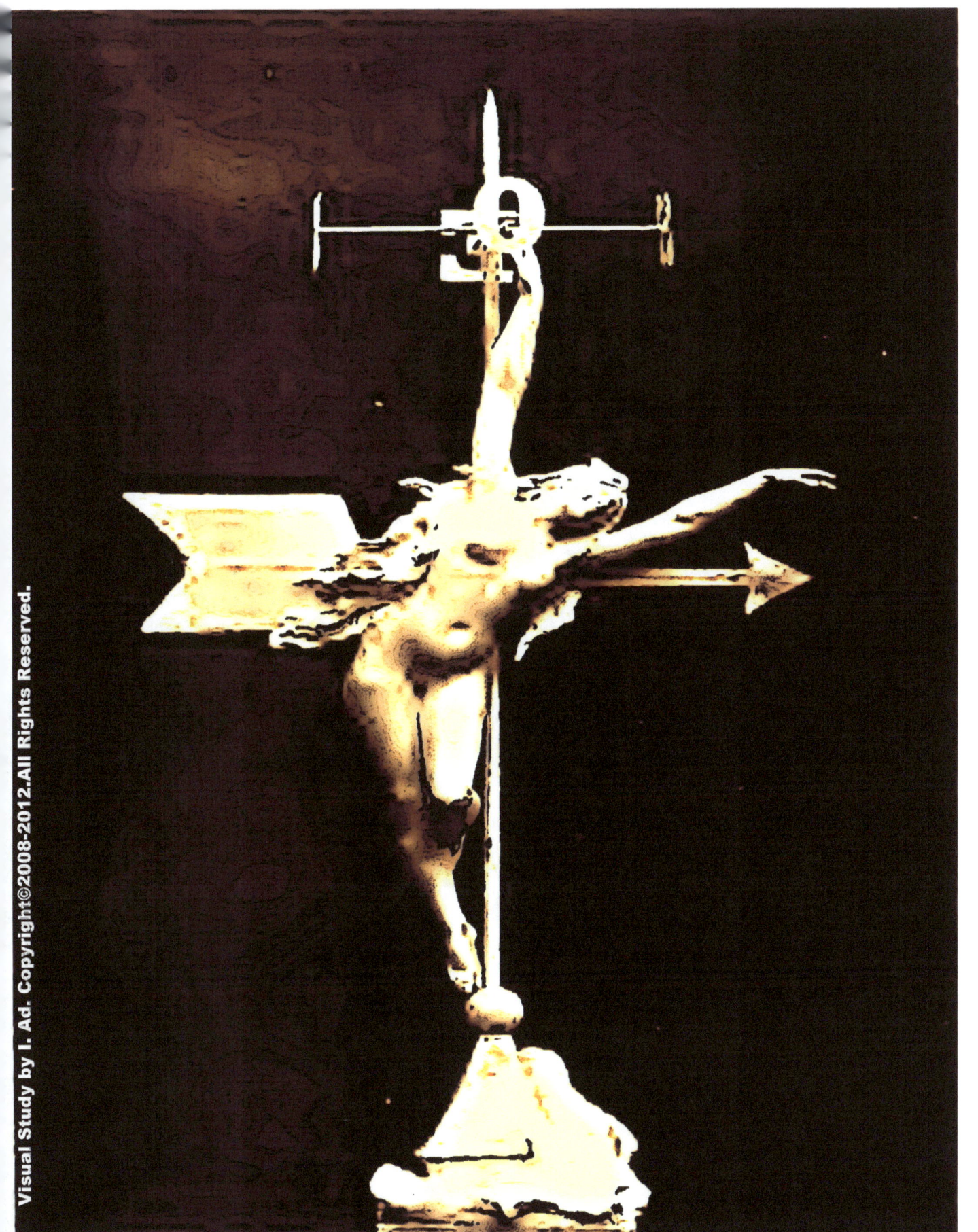

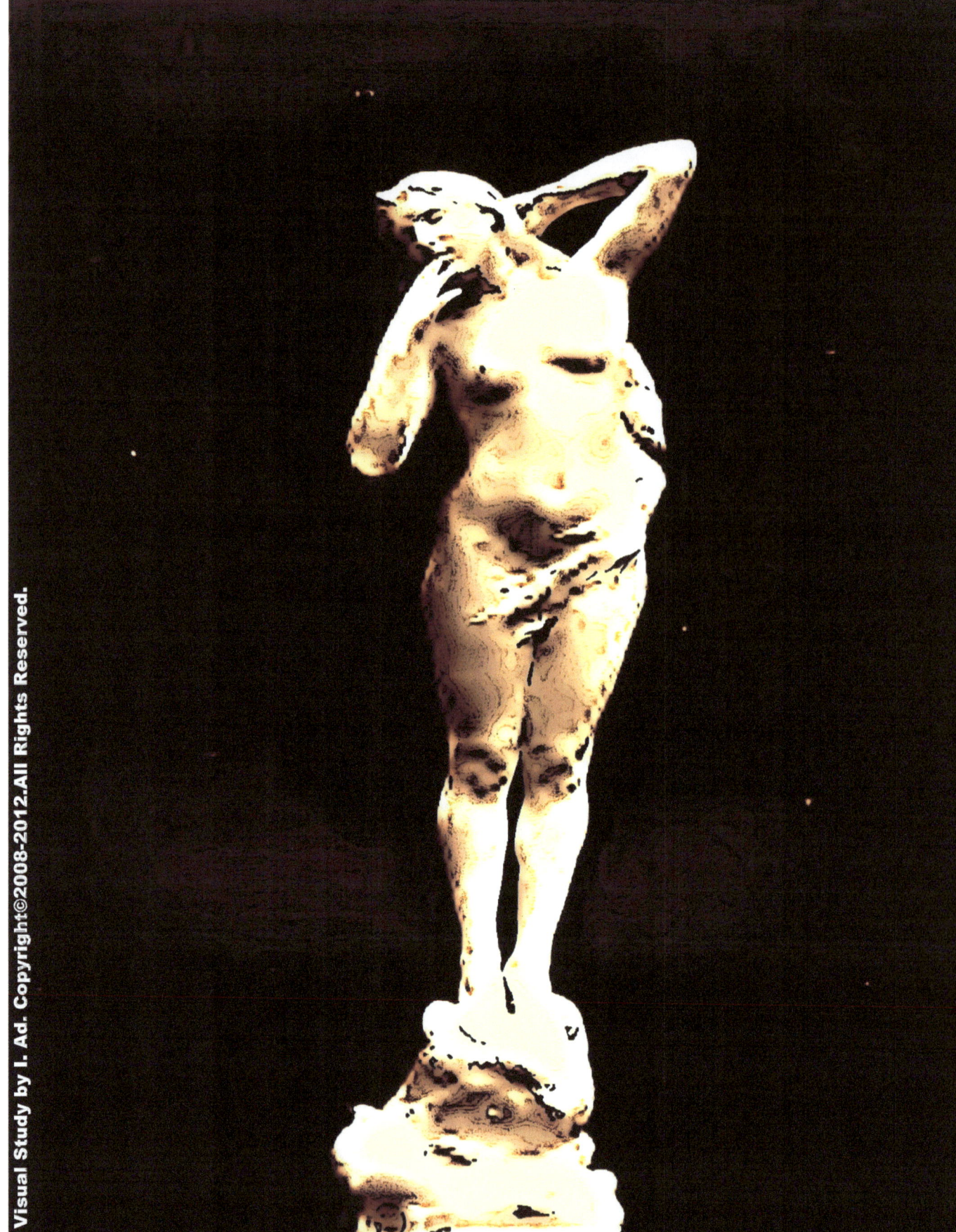

Bibliographic sources :

Le Nu au salon (1888)

Author : Silvestre, Armand, 1837-1901 ;
            Société nationale des beaux-arts (France). Salon ;
            Société des artistes français. Salon.
Volume: 14 .